Mathematics and the Primary Curriculum

MESU

Microelectronics Education Support Unit

First published 1988 by
MESU (Microelectronics Education Support Unit)
Unit 6
Sir William Lyons Road
Science Park
University of Warwick
Coventry CV4 7EZ

ISBN 1 85379 023 0

Printed by Quorn Selective Repro Ltd., Queens Road, Loughborough, Leics. LE11 1HH.

Contents

Acknowledgements

MESU would like to acknowledge the time and effort of the following people in planning, preparing and working to produce these materials.

MESU Coordinators:	Jenny Brown, Janice Staines
Editors:	Katrina Blythe, Sharon Harrison

Working Group:

Ken Brown	N.E.W.I, Cartrefle College, Wrexham
Brenda Butler	Walsall LEA
Susan Cameron	Charlotte Mason College, Ambleside, Cumbria
Ros Foot	Devon LEA
Jeff Goodwin	PrIME Project, Homerton College, Cambridge
Lynda Maple	BEAM Project, William Tyndale Maths Centre, London
Jacky Moore	Newham LEA
Alan Parr	Hertfordshire LEA
Derek Peasey	Retired teacher
Chris Robinson	Croydon LEA
Jenny Saady	Oxfordshire LEA
Janet Shakespeare	Cambridgeshire LEA
John Teago	Coventry LEA
Phil Waite	Gloucestershire LEA
Angie Walsh	PrIME Project, Homerton College, Cambridge
Steve Wright	Newham LEA

Preface

This reader highlights the important issues in primary mathematics and sets the scene for the other reader, *The Impact of New Technology on the Primary Mathematics Curriculum,*

It is intended for primary information technology advisory teachers, who may not be mathematics specialists, but will be required to work in the area of primary mathematics and IT as part of their overall support. The two readers could also be of interest to advisory teachers in primary mathematics, mathematics coordinators in primary and middle schools and college lecturers.

Introduction

This is the first booklet in a series of four:

Mathematics and the Primary Curriculum
The Impact of New Technology on the Primary Mathematics Curriculum
New Technology in Primary Mathematics: Classroom Accounts
New Technology in Primary Mathematics: INSET Resources

The booklet focuses on the model of the primary mathematics curriculum, described by Hilary Shuard in *Primary Mathematics Today and Tomorrow*. This sees the curriculum comprising four central strands:

* content - facts, skills and concepts
* processes
* children's appreciation and attitudes
* situations within which learning and teaching take place

It looks at the place of mathematics within the primary curriculum where, despite the similarities of processes involved, links are often not made and mathematics is seen in isolation. While children can frequently be seen solving problems and working in an investigational way in other areas of the curriculum, this is not always the case in mathematics. This booklet suggests ways of starting and developing this way of working.

There are many advantages to developing mathematics within a cross-curricular theme and a flexible approach to mathematics should include some work of this nature. Three themes with a varying degree of mathematical content are presented.

Lastly the booklet looks at the role new technology can play in linking mathematics across the primary curriculum and in helping to develop a problem-solving and investigational approach. This serves as an introduction to booklet 2 where this is developed more fully.

Setting the Context

The natural learning style of young children . . .

'The child is curious. He wants to make sense out of things, find out how things work, gain competence and control over himself and his environment, do what he can see other people doing. He is open, receptive and perceptive. He observes the world around him closely and sharply, tries to take it all in. He is experimental. He does not merely observe the world around him but tastes it, touches it, bends it, breaks it. He is bold. He is not afraid of making mistakes. And he is patient.'

J. Holt, *How Children Learn*

. . . the demands of a changing society

'We live in a changing society, a society that is making increasing demands on the problem-solving skills of its citizens. The school curriculum is also changing in response to these new demands. Emphasis is moving away from the transmission of facts, the products of knowledge neatly packaged into special subject areas, towards an approach which focuses on the process of study, investigation and problem-solving. This approach moves from simply teaching children the facts of language, mathematics, history, geography, science and the other "disciplines", towards encouraging children to be scientists, historians, geographers, linguists and mathematicians through the use of appropriate problem-solving skills and processes.'

R. Fisher, *Problem-Solving in Primary Schools*

A Model for Describing Primary Mathematics

The following article develops a model for describing the primary mathematics curriculum. When we think about primary mathematics it is tempting to think only of the content of the curriculum and not to give enough thought to factors such as the teaching styles used, the technology that is available to the children, and the environment and social context of the school. The model is intended to assist in balanced thinking about the many features that contribute to primary mathematics. The article is taken from *Primary Mathematics Today and Tomorrow* by Hilary Shuard published by Longman for the School Curriculum Development Committee.

The Cockcroft Report calls attention, in paras 240-1, to the fact that effective mathematics teaching needs to attend to a number of different elements of mathematics:

facts
skills
conceptual structures
general strategies for problem-solving and investigation
appreciation of the nature of mathematics
attitudes towards mathematics

When a particular mathematics curriculum is described, it is very common for only the first three of these elements - facts, skills, and conceptual structures - to be listed. These elements form the *content* of primary mathematics. The other listed elements tend not to be explicitly described in the documentation of a curriculum, except in the most general terms. General strategies for problem-solving and investigation are especially difficult to describe, and it is, therefore, important to try to describe them as fully as possible so that they are not overlooked in curriculum building. These strategies form part of a range of *processes* involved in doing mathematics, and consequently should form an important part of children's mathematical education.

Another important feature of primary mathematics is the fact that, for children, mathematics is set in the context of a variety of situations and experiences, and is built upon these situations and experiences, some of which are found in the children's environment and some of which are contrived by the teacher. There needs to be a constant interplay between these *situations* and the mathematical ideas the children are learning if they are to be able to apply their mathematics to everyday situations.

Hence, three important dimensions of the primary mathematics curriculum are the *content*, *processes,* and *situations* of primary mathematics. All three of these dimensions need to be considered in documenting or building a curriculum. So, too, does a fourth dimension concerned with children's *appreciation* of mathematics and their *attitudes* towards it, which need to permeate all the mathematics that is done in school. In Figure 1, these four dimensions of the mathematics curriculum are shown as the four faces of a tetrahedron. The front face, which represents *appreciation* and *attitudes*, is cut away to reveal the three faces representing *processes, content,* and *situations.*

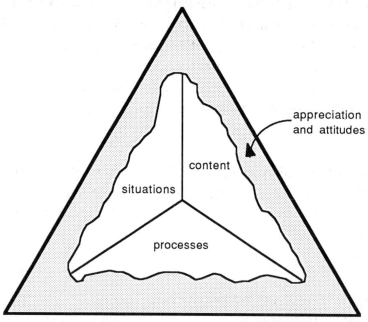

Figure 1 The primary mathematics curriculum

Thus, any particular mathematical experience which the curriculum provides (such as finding the volume of a small box) can be looked at in terms of the content it embodies (the concept of volume), the processes which children use (perhaps making a practical experiment by filling it with sand, or creating a mathematical model by first measuring its dimensions), and the situation from which it came (in this case probably a situation contrived by the teacher to give experience of volume). Finally, the children bring to the experience attitudes such as interest in what they are doing and confidence that they will succeed (or perhaps the opposite).

These four dimensions can be thought of both as inputs to the experience, as suggested above, and as outputs: through the experience, the children will strengthen their concept of volume, become more able to create mathematical models, and become more aware of experimental situations embodying volume. Their experience will also strengthen or contribute to changing their attitudes and appreciation of mathematics.

The Wider Context

However, this model does not contain all the factors which need to be taken into account in curriculum building. The curriculum is conveyed to the pupils by the teacher's *style of teaching* and is expressed in the resulting organisation of the classroom work. These enable the curriculum to be put into practice, and through them the aims on which the curriculum is based are realised. For instance, only if the teacher is able to present mathematics to the pupils as 'a powerful means of communication' (*Cockcroft*, para. 3) can the pupils be expected to realise that it is so.

Furthermore, curriculum building must take into account *how pupils learn*. It is useless to build a curriculum if pupils are unable to understand and learn the mathematics contained in it. Much of the evidence accumulated by the *APU* (1980, 1981, 1982) and by the *Concepts in Secondary Mathematics and Science Project* (Hart, 1981) in this country, and by the *National Assessment of Educational Progress* in the USA (Lindquist *et al.*, 1983) indicates that many pupils are not very successful in learning mathematics from the present primary curriculum. The evidence is not all negative; valuable information is accumulating about ways in which children spontaneously think about mathematics, about children's informal methods of calculation, and about their personal problem-solving strategies. If the curriculum can be structured so as to respect and build upon children's own thinking rather than ignoring it, as often happens when the detail of their thinking is not known, then the curriculum may be more effective in producing learning and understanding.

Next, the primary mathematics curriculum is at least partially dependent on the *technology* available for use. In some cultures, especially in the Orient, until very recently, the technology of primary mathematics has been based on the abacus. In our own culture, throughout the last hundred years, the technology of primary mathematics has been based on pencil and paper. Children have needed to learn the algorithms of pencil-and-paper arithmetic, and to draw graphs on paper, because these technologies were the only ones available. Now the arrival of new technology means that primary children can use calculators to perform arithmetical operations of a complexity they could not previously handle, and the computer screen can display not only bar graphs but also pie charts, the calculations for which were too complex for many children to undertake at the primary stage.

Finally, the primary mathematics curriculum must take account of the larger contexts of *society* and *schooling*. A curriculum which is unacceptable to the children's parents, to the governors of their schools, and to the public is bound to fail, because schools will be unable to carry it into practice in the face of criticism and opposition. This is not to say that the larger community cannot be influenced to espouse a cause such as that of curriculum development in mathematics, but this context cannot be ignored. *The Cockcroft Report* was almost universally well received, both within education and without, and post-

Cockcroft development of the primary mathematics curriculum might be expected to attract considerable support. However, because many adults have a narrow conception of mathematics, and negative attitudes towards it, it is important to work to help parents to understand the reasons that curriculum development is needed, the directions it should take, and their own necessary part in their children's mathematical education.

Similarly, the *school* context needs to be considered.\If the teaching styles used in mathematics are not consonant with those used in other curriculum areas, or if different teachers have different philosophies, then the pupils will be confused. For example, if one teacher expects pupils to think mathematically for themselves while the next year another teacher tells those same pupils to learn the rules and not worry about reasons for them, then the pupils cannot know whether mathematics is concerned with thinking and communication, or whether it is a set of procedures carried out by arbitrary rules. Thus, the context in which it is possible for the curriculum to operate within a particular school must be taken into account in developing a curriculum for that school. Figure 2 depicts all these influences on primary mathematics.

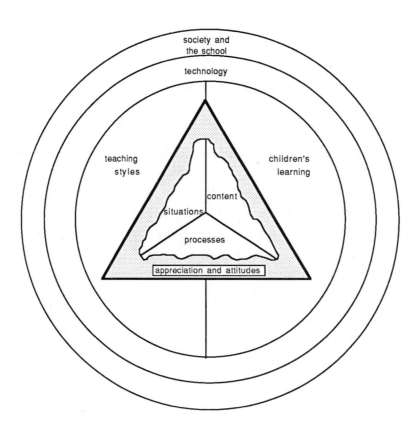

Figure 2: A model of primary mathematics for curriculum building

Perceptions of Mathematics

Children's perceptions of mathematics depend largely upon the experiences they have at school and consequently they are very different.

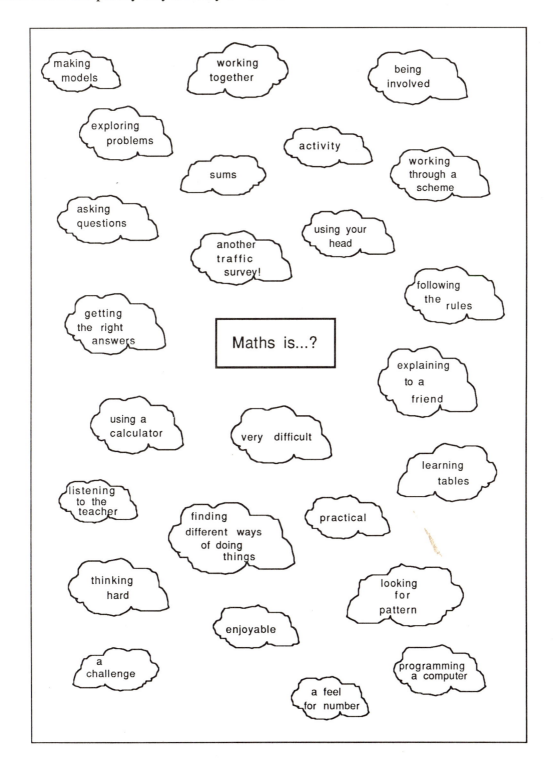

Figure 1: Children's different perceptions of mathematics

Adults views show a similar diversity. The teacher has to be alert to this.

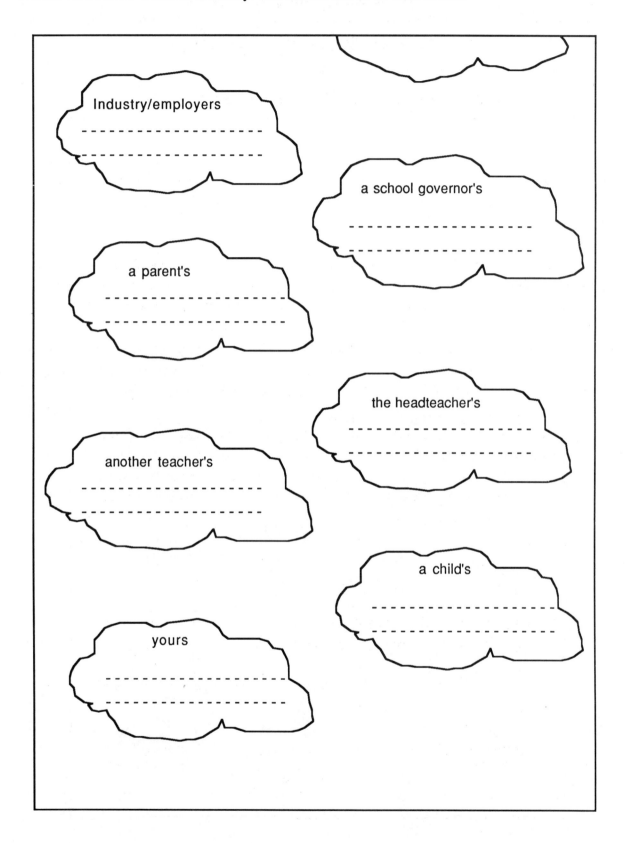

Figure 2: Different people's perceptions of mathematics

Children as Empty Vessels
v
Children as Mathematical Thinkers

It is easy to view children as needing 'filling' with mathematical knowledge and skills. This can be thought of as the child being 'an empty vessel' into which you pour mathematics. As all of us know, children are very 'leaky' containers! This is particularly apparent following a summer holiday!

It is not sufficient for children to have some knowledge of mathematical facts, concepts, and skills. They also need to be able to put their knowledge to work. The additional abilities required to do this are referred to as the processes of mathematical activity.

Children who are thinking mathematically are actively engaged in constructing mathematical knowledge for themselves. They are using mathematical processes and 'doing mathematics'. In this way, skills and knowledge are being assimilated.

Mathematicians view their subject as a searching/finding/proving/searching one.
Each journey around the search/find/prove track results in a fragment of
mathematical knowledge being established and a new set of tracks being revealed.
So mathematics is both a body of established, recognised content and a process
by which exploration and establishing takes place.

There is mathematics to know
and mathematics to do.

To be involved in mathematics, at whatever level, requires both content and process, otherwise the subject is being experienced in an unbalanced way.

L. Burton, *Problem-solving in Primary Schools*

classifying   **refining**   **questioning**

predicting   **explaining**   **proving**   **reflecting**

The maths processes described in books use words like generalising, hypothesising, specialising etc. . . . and as a class teacher, I was never aware that these processes were happening in my class. I needed an interpreter.

Throughout the day the children were playing, exploring, talking, sorting, guessing etc. in order to solve problems, but I did not realise that such activities were processes which the children were developing while applying the understanding and skills acquired in the maths lesson.

- an ESG Advisory Teacher for Mathematics

imaging   **describing**   **generalising**

specialising   **discussing**   **conjecturing**

Figure 1: Processes of mathematical activity

Think back to your experiences of school days:

How were you taught mathematics?

Think back to the last time you did a mathematical activity yourself:

How do you learn mathematics?

Think back to the last time you worked with children:

How do you teach mathematics?

Figure 2: Your perceptions of mathematics

Problem-Solving and Investigation

The Cockcroft Committee regarded problem-solving and investigation as central activities in mathematics. A close relationship exists between the two.

> Clear distinctions do not exist between problem-solving and investigative work. Nevertheless, in broad terms, it is useful to think of problem-solving as being a convergent activity where the pupils have to reach a solution to a defined problem, whereas investigative work should be seen as a more divergent activity. In an investigative approach pupils are encouraged to think of alternative strategies, to consider what would happen if a particular line of action were pursued, or to see whether certain changes would make any difference to the outcome. In fact, it might be through an investigative approach to a problem that a solution emerged.

> DES, *Mathematics from 5 to 16*

The processes of mathematical activity include general strategies for problem-solving and investigation. It is as important that children should learn to use these general strategies as it is that they should learn the facts, skills, and conceptual structures of maths. Such strategies, however, are often barely touched on in maths teaching, and pupils are left to discover them for themselves.

The article on the following page is from *Maths Teaching, 120*, and describes how a number of children of widely differing ages worked on a problem which highlights mathematical processes. Such an activity not only focuses children's attention on the processes but also helps in the development of their problem-solving and investigational strategies.

Levels of Knowing 2
'The Handshake',
Jeannie Billington and Pat Evans

In the end it took me three hours, the answer was get the two numbers like a 100, 99 times them, get your answer and half it and there is the result.

THE END

BY DEAN (aged 10)

Dean's written words in no way convey the sheer joy and delight he expressed at the time of his discovery. The surge of excitement which he experienced is an important part of knowing. What happened at that moment of discovery? What mental processes were taking place? What did he see with his inner eye?

Dean had been working on a variation of the following problem: There were seven people at a party. If everyone shook hands with everyone else once and once only, how many handshakes would there be?

The 'handshake problem' is a very simple one and can be used at many different levels, from a purely practical problem for young children through to generalising and providing the results for *n* people. We have worked on the problem with many children whose ages range from 6 to 15.

Factors influencing the children's success

Children demonstrated through the 'handshake problem' several levels of knowing. Their ability to do so was influenced by three external variables:
* the nature and presentation of the problem; a tangible aspect
* the general strategies used by the children; a less tangible aspect
* the role of the teacher

The nature and presentation of the problem

The 'handshake problem' appeared to enable children to get an answer, find a rule and know why the rule works. There were those children who found an answer and were convinced, with varying levels of confidence, that their answer was right! Some children, not content with finding an answer, went on to search for a rule which would work for any number of people shaking hands. There were interesting levels of sophistication in the development of the rule. Ultimately there were those children who could see why the rule worked.

General strategies used by the children

We were intrigued by the general strategies the children used. *The Cockcroft Report* describes general strategies as 'procedures which guide the choice of which skills to use or what knowledge to draw upon at each stage in the course of solving a problem or carrying out an investigation. They enable a problem to be approached with confidence and with the expectation that a solution will be possible'. There was evidence, at different levels of the 'handshake problem', of children's ability to:
- process information and 'own' the problem
- make predictions and test them
- symbolise
- tabulate
- illustrate their mental pictures and/or physical actions by diagrams
- search for and investigate patterns
- see connections
- generalise
- establish a proof

It seemed that a combination of some of these abilities enabled the children to find solutions.

The role of the teacher

The role of the teacher is crucial in the 'enabling'. We are convinced that some, if not all, of the general strategies listed above are natural to children and should be developed not taught. Children need to know that their ideas are not only acceptable but encouraged. Allowing time and space for children to develop and test their own predictions is essential.

We have recorded the children's work under the following headings: getting an answer, finding a rule, and knowing why the rule works. We have tried to demonstrate the strategies that the children are using. The work is mainly of two age groups: second-year juniors and fourth-year secondary.

The children were introduced to the problem orally. They were encouraged to work collaboratively, sharing and developing their own ideas and those of others. Although the younger children worked collaboratively, they tended to write up their solutions individually and in their own time. The older children wrote group solutions. They were expected from the beginning to generalise the situation, e.g. 'How many handshakes for seven people, twenty-seven people, *n* number of people?'

Processing
Information

Tabulating

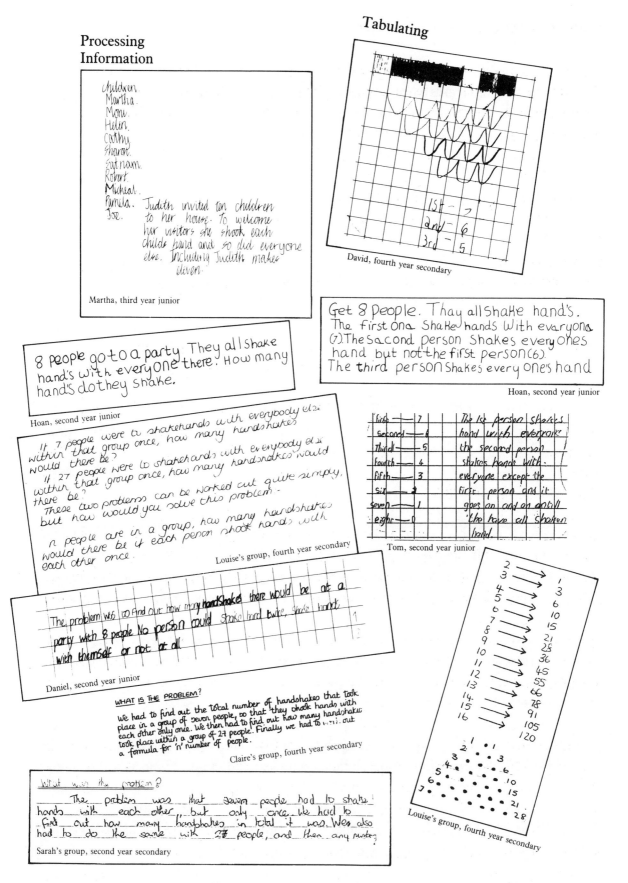

children.
Martha.
Moru.
Helen.
Cathy.
Sharon.
Eatnam.
Robert.
Micheal.
Pamela.
Joe.

Judith invited ten children to her house. To welcome her visitors she shook each childs hand and so did everyone else. Including Judith makes eleven.

Martha, third year junior

David, fourth year secondary

Get 8 people. Thay all shake hand's. The first one shake hands with everyone (7). The second person shakes every ones hand but not the first person (6). The third person shakes every one's hand

Hoan, second year junior

8 people go to a party They all shake hand's with everyone there. How many hand's do they shake.

Hoan, second year junior

If 7 people were to shakehands with everybody else within that group once, how many handshakes would there be?
If 27 people were to shakehands with everybody else within that group once, how many handshakes would there be?
These two problems can be worked out quite simply, but how would you solve this problem.
n people are in a group, how many handshakes would there be if each person shook hands with each other once.

Louise's group, fourth year secondary

first	—	7	The 1st person shakes
Second	—	6	hand with everyone
Third	—	5	the second person
fourth	—	4	shakes hands with.
fifth	—	3	everyone except the
six	—	2	first person and it
seven	—	1	goes on and on antill
eight	—	0	the have all shaken hand.

Tom, second year junior

The problem was to find out how many handshakes there would be at a party with 8 people No person could shake hand twice, shake hands with themself or not at all

Daniel, second year junior

WHAT IS THE PROBLEM?
We had to find out the total number of handshakes that took place in a group of seven people, so that they shook hands with each other only once. We then had to find out how many handshakes took place within a group of 27 people. Finally we had to [...] out a formula for 'n' number of people.

Claire's group, fourth year secondary

What was the problem?
The problem was that seven people had to shake hands with each other, but only once. We had to find out how many handshakes in total it was. We also had to do the same with 27 people, and then any number

Sarah's group, second year secondary

Louise's group, fourth year secondary

Figure 1: Getting an answer

Getting an answer

Processing information and 'owning' the problem
The children needed to clarify certain points. The younger children, in particular, asked the following types of question:
What's a handshake?
Do you have to shake hands with everybody?
Do you shake hands with yourself?
Can you shake hands more than once?
If I shake hands with Marlon is that one handshake or two?

Once the boundaries of the problem were clearly defined they began to make predictions. The older children, plus a few younger ones, made predictions immediately.

We did not, at this stage, ask the children to describe the problem in their own words. However, we are including some of the children's descriptions of the problem taken from their written solutions. It is interesting to see how individuals or groups interpreted the problem.

Daniel's 'text-book' description of the problem was very sophisticated. He was quick, when the problem was first posed, to establish the basic parameters by asking a few pertinent questions. Hence the statement in his second sentence. His solution and extension of the problem were more elaborate than those of any other child in his age group. Martha found it necessary to weave a story around the problem and to use real characters. It was Hoan's first attempt at problem-solving. Although successful, she was the only child who did not symbolise or use diagrams. She was new to the school and we presume had not been encouraged to 'problem solve' before. We always encourage our children to use apparatus or draw diagrams to help them. The older children's descriptions were, as expected, much more advanced.

Making and testing their predictions

Many hunches were plucked out of the air as being immediate solutions. The older children tended to use algebraic expressions. Some obvious predictions were made. We heard:

'It's n^2'	'It's $2n$'	'8!'
'It's 8 x 8'	'It's 8 x 2'	'8 x 7'
'It's 64'	'It's 16'	'56!'

A period of intense activity followed. The hunches seemed to have been forgotten amidst this activity, but the children returned to them once they had reached the stage of finding a rule.

Symbolising

The children surprised us by using a wide variety of symbols. They included combinations of the following: colour, dots, letters of the alphabet, names, numbers, objects (e.g. unifix), 'pin' people, and the children themselves.

Tabulating

The symbolising seemed to develop into tabulating. There were two types of tabulation: one related to solving the first part of the problem, e.g., eight people at a party, and the other related to extending the problem to other numbers of people. It was interesting to observe those children who included one person - nil handshakes. Daniel was the only second-year junior child to explore beyond the first part of the problem. He did so of his own accord. However, he was not prepared to investigate further than producing his table.

1 person	– 0	handshakes
2 people	– 1	handshakes
3 people	– 3	handshakes
4 people	– 6	handshakes
5 people	– 10	handshakes
6 people	– 15	handshakes
7 people	– 21	handshakes
8 people	– 28	handshakes
9 people	– 36	handshakes
10 people	– 45	handshakes

Figure 2: Illustrating their mental pictures and/or physical actions with diagrams

The majority of younger children needed to solve the problem physically. They either arranged themselves in groups and actually shook hands or they used real objects such as unifix. Some of these younger children began to work out the problem using themselves but found the task frustrating because a few would not stand still. They reverted to using objects or drawing diagrams. The older children tended to visualise the problem mentally from the start and depicted their mental images on paper.

We were astounded, at first, by the similarity between the diagrams drawn by the younger and older children. However, we realised on reflection that certain problems lend themselves to the use of certain diagrams, such as networks and mappings, which both appeared. The younger children tended to reinforce their diagrams with colours and names. These factors generally were absent from the older children's work. Daniel, once again, was the only junior child to use a 'graph'.

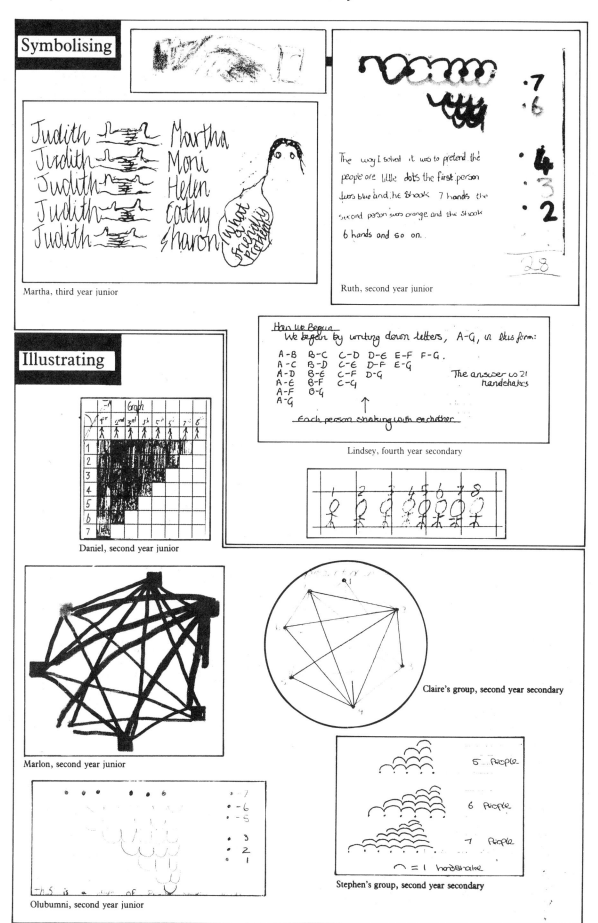

Symbolising

Judith
Judith
Judith
Judith
Judith

Martha
Moni
Helen
Cathy
Sharon

What a friendly problem!

Martha, third year junior

The way I solved it was to pretend the people are little dots the first person was blue and he shook 7 hands the second person was orange and she shook 6 hands and so on.

·7
·6
·4
·3
·2

28

Ruth, second year junior

Illustrating

Graph

	1st	2nd	3rd	4th	5th	6th	7th	8th
1								
2								
3								
4								
5								
6								
7								

Daniel, second year junior

How We Begin
We began by writing down letters, A-G, in this form:

A-B B-C C-D D-E E-F F-G
A-C B-D C-E D-F E-G
A-D B-E C-F D-G
A-E B-F C-G
A-F B-G
A-G

The answer is 21 handshakes

↑

Each person shaking with each other

Lindsey, fourth year secondary

Marlon, second year junior

Claire's group, second year secondary

This is a of

Olubumni, second year junior

5 PEOPLE

6 PEOPLE

7 PEOPLE

∩ = 1 handshake

Stephen's group, second year secondary

Searching for and investigating patterns

Through the development of the diagrams, patterns began to emerge. Most children, regardless of age, spotted the consecutive number pattern. For the younger ones, this was as far as they were prepared to go. They were able to explain, when questioned, that with 19 people, for example, there would be 18 + 17 + 16 + 15 . . . handshakes. They were rather pleased with themselves and had had enough for one day. The older children went on to investigate different numbers of people. Several of them spotted the triangular number pattern, but none of them investigated the differences between the triangular numbers. They used other methods to find a rule and proof. This is particularly interesting when most mathematical text books emphasize these differences. One very able second-year junior child, Ruth, did use differences to establish a rule. Her work is included under the 'Finding a Rule' section.

All the children who persevered with the problem found an answer to the first part of it. Using real objects or their mathematical diagrams, they were able to convince themselves and others of the 'correctness' of their answers. This gave them a great sense of satisfaction and creativity. They could do it! For some of the older children it had taken a matter of minutes. For others it had been a much longer, and in some cases, arduous task. Marlon, for example, needed to reinforce his understanding of the problem by explaining his solution to his friends and his class teacher, by using unifix, before it really clicked. As a child who can hardly read or write, he was very proud of his final diagram. All of the children had a sense of achievement, to a lesser or greater degree depending on how tortuous their route had been and how secure they were in knowing that they were right.

Finding a rule

Generalising
The confidence gained from finding the 'correct' answer to the first part of the problem gave some children the incentive to generalise and make predictions for other numbers and situations. There were various levels of sophistication in their attempts to do so. These levels can be categorised as follows:

• Seeing the consecutive number pattern

• Seeing the triangular number pattern

• Finding a logical explanation

• Finding an algebraic explanation

Most children spotted the consecutive number pattern but there were differences in the degree of confidence shown by children in applying this understanding to other numbers.

Finding a rule
Generalising

Ruth's algorithm:

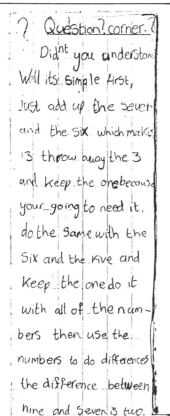

? Question? corner. ?
Didn't you understand
Well its simple first,
just add up the seven
and the six which makes
13 throw away the 3
and keep the one because
your going to need it,
do the same with the
six and the five and
keep the one do it
with all of the num-
bers then use the
numbers to do differences
the difference between
nine and seven is two,
the seven and five, two, five and three
two and the difference between one and one
is nothing. Now we know were got the two
then add up the four twos which make eight.

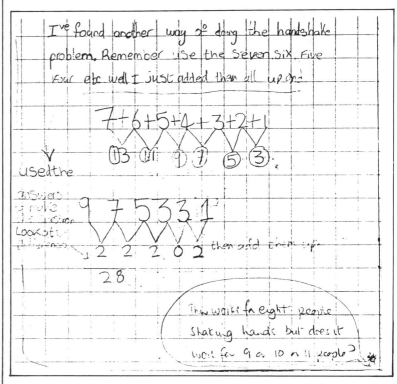

I've found another way of doing the handshake problem. Remember use the seven six, five four etc well I just added them all up and

7+6+5+4+3+2+1
13 11   9 7   5 3

used the
answers to make the
decision
look at the
differences

9 7 5 3 3 1
2 2 2 0 2   then add them up.
28

This works for eight people shaking hands but does it work for 9 or 10 or 11 people?

Dean's algorithm:

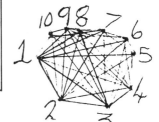

AND THIS HOW YOU DISPLAY IT IN WRITING

The number what is out lined is total amount
of lines in the display, but in
Telecom the dots would be houses and
the lines would be cables.
When I finished 10 dots I went and did 50 dots then
150 TO 200 dots and my

results are on the sheet of paper next to this.
Then I showed miss billington and she said can you think
of a quick way of doing it?
so I went out to play , when I came in I started to
write.
In the end it took me three hours, the answer was
Get the two top numbers like a 100 99
times them, get your answer
and half it.
and there is the result.

              THE END
                  BY DEAN

1=9
2=8
3=7
4=6
5=5
6=4
7=3
8=2
9=1

45

When Shaun, age 8, was asked if it would work for any number, he suggested:

S: Well get them all in a row - it doesn't matter how big, and the person at the top goes down the row shaking hands. Well, he has to do the number of people less one because he can't shake hands with himself. Then he goes away from the room and the next person gets going. He can't have done it before with anyone otherwise he'd have to get out of line. So his number of handshakes is one less than the first one. If you keep it up you will be left with only one person who hasn't got anyone else and you are finished.'

T: 'Would it work for even one million?' (very stupid question)

S: 'Well I don't know. I don't think so.'

T: 'Why? You said it would work for all numbers.'

S: 'Well the line would be too long and people would get fed up waiting for a shake.'

Shaun knew the method would work but had qualms about people getting bored. The fourteen-year olds did not have this problem. Their certainty showed itself in the following formula:

n people = $(n-1) + (n-2) + (n-3) + (n-4) + (n-5) + (n-6) + (n-7)$ .... until $n-(n-1)$

Some children spotted the triangular number pattern:

1 person	-	0 handshakes
2 people	-	1 handshake
3 people	-	3 handshakes
4 people	-	6 handshakes

However, this was not particularly helpful in finding the ultimate formula. The older children realised this and the problem began to change. It became 'how do you find the sum of the first n natural numbers? A lull followed this change. The lull was vital. Children began to try out ideas and play with them. At this stage it was very important to give them time and space. In short they were 'stuck', and it was difficult to watch and wait without interfering. If they were to reach their own level of knowing, it was important to allow them to select their own route. There are times when it is necessary to intervene, but this was not one of them. It took Dean (aged 10) three hours. His class had been doing a project on communication. They had been studying British Telecom services. The 'handshake problem' became the 'houses and cables' problem. Dean was fascinated by the patterns that emerged and had worked hard to determine the number of cables needed for 200 homes. He eventually found a logical solution. He was thrilled. The fourteen-year olds, after playing with summing numbers and trying out rules, generally came back to the structure of the problem itself, and solutions began to emerge.

Sarah's group generated:

the rule $\underline{n^2\text{-}n}$ or $\underline{n(n\text{-}1)}$ both these work

       2   2

Stephen's group formulated:

We derived two rules:

$\dfrac{n^2 - n}{2}$ = no. of handshakes $\dfrac{n - 1}{2} \times n$ = no. of handshakes

Although the solutions are clear, the processes by which they are reached them are not. Some children went half way to discovering the rule and made the rest fit. Lindsey's group did just that:

Ruth, age 9, solved the problem quite easily at school. Then during the half-term holiday, she watched a maths programme on television. She told me the programme was exploring the differences between some number patterns. This inspired her to find another way of solving the problem. She developed a complicated algorithm which works in the case of eight children shaking hands. She did not explore it any further than that until I talked to her about it.

Knowing why the rule works

Establishing a Proof
Some of the older children were not content to find a rule. Encouraged by the teacher they went on to prove why the rule works.

Levels of knowing

The sense of achievement felt by the children was very real. The confidence they gained from knowing they had 'cracked' the first part of the problem gave them the incentive to continue. There seemed to be surges of energy and excitement followed by lulls and some frustration. These aspects of problem-solving and investigational work are often overlooked. The relief and excitement of knowing are not seen very often in the classroom because teachers tend not to put themselves or the children at risk.

Knowing why the rule works
Establishing a Proof

The proof from Claire's group

THE RULE!

When we had worked out how many handshakes took place within a group of 7, we then worked out how many it would take if everyone shook hands twice. From this we got the equation: $n(n-1)$. This was, however, wrong. But from this wrong equation we worked out the right answer, with everybody shaking hands just once. This turned out to be half of the first answer, so we halved the equation, making our final version:

$$\frac{n(n-1)}{2}$$

THE PROOF?

We took the equation $\frac{n^2 - n}{2}$ and drew this chart out:

The method we used to draw this chart, representing the 7 people who shake hands with each other, was as follows: As person 1 cannot shake hands with himself (i.e. person 1), we drew a nought on that square. We continued this pattern for person 2 and 2, 3 and 3, etc. All the squares where there would be a handshake, we ticked on the chart, eg. 1 and 2, 1 and 3, etc. All the remaining squares, we put a cross in them, representing that no handshake took place, because they had already had a handshake, eg. we had ticked square (1,2) so a cross was put against square (2,1). The squares with ticks in were counted, giving us our total number of handshakes. Our finished chart proved that our formula worked:

formula: $\frac{n^2}{2}$ (our chart numbers: 7 people x 7 people.) $-n$ (minus the 7 noughts where no handshake took place.) $\div 2$ (divided by 2 because out of the noughts and ticks only the ticks involve a handshake.)

reason:

David and Jonathan's proof

The problem was to find a solution to be able to work out the amount of handshakes needed for any number of people in a group to shake hands with each other. This was to be done without having to use diagrams each time but with the aid of just one equation.
For example!

A group of people contains seven members. Find the number of hand shakes required for each member of the group to shake hands with each other member once only.

One way to work this out would be to use the following system!

members of group = A, B, C, D, E, F, G

AB	BC	CD	DE	EF	FG
AC	BD	CE	DF	EG	
AD	BE	CF	DG		
AE	BF	CG			
AF	BG				
AG					

Total of handshakes required = 21

The above system is how we began our investigation.

To work out an equation for this we started by realising the fact that the maximum number of handshakes required would be the number of people in the group squared. In the case above this would be!

$$7^2 = 49$$

We then realised that the members of the group would not shake hands with themselves so we took away the amount of members in the group from the total of members squared. From this we arrived at!

$$7^2 - 7 = 42$$

After this we realised that each member had to shake hands with each other member ONCE ONLY so one member "a" had shook hands with member "b" it was not necessary for member "b" to shake hands with member "a".
Because of this we decided that it was necessary to half the amount of hand shakes required. From this we came to the equation!

$$\frac{7^2 - 7}{2} = 21$$

For this to work with any number of given people in a group, we replaced the number "7" with the letter "n" and came to the final equation of!

$$\frac{n^2 - n}{2}$$

Proof that this equation works is illustrated in the diagram below!

O	A	B	C	D	E	F
A	O	O	O	O	O	O
B	X	O	O	O	O	O
C	X	X	O	O	O	O
D	X	X	X	O	O	O
E	X	X	X	X	O	O
F	X	X	X	X	X	O
G						

O = Necessary handshakes

X = Unnecessary hand shakes

The proof from Louise's group

To find this we used different methods and some of these we have shown.

We started off by using an equation
eg
$$n \text{ people: } (n-1)+(n-2)+(n-3)+(n-4)+(n-5)+(n-6)+(n-7) \text{ etc until } n-(n-1)$$

When we shortened this the formula was four of course we had to see if this was true and so by using the above methods we found the proof of the problem.
With the triangle each added layer gave the next number of handshakes. We tried the formula with other given numbers which worked.
eg $\frac{64^2 - 64}{2} = \frac{4096 - 64}{2} = 2016$.

If we worked this out with a triangle we would get the same result but the method is much longer.

The triangle method works like this:-

You have a square which represents N^2

You cut the square into two triangles, this represents the $\div 2$

The blank triangle represents N. This means so far the formula is $N^2 - N$

The two triangles then complete the formula by representing the $\div 2$.
So this means $\frac{n^2 - n}{2}$ the formula

to find an alternative method
This is what we came up with..
THE RULE
$$n^2(-n \div 2) =$$
$$\frac{n^2 - n}{2}$$

We came to this conclusion – use this

2 ⟶	1
3 ⟶	3
4 ⟶	6
5 ⟶	10
6 ⟶	15
7 ⟶	21
8 ⟶	28
9 ⟶	36
10 ⟶	45
11 ⟶	55
12 ⟶	66
13 ⟶	78
14 ⟶	91
15 ⟶	105
16 ⟶	120

using 5 as the first example.

$$\frac{5^2 - 5}{2} = \frac{25 - 5}{2} = \frac{20}{2}$$

$$= 10.$$

This works out for all the other numbers.

We also found that this can be represented by a triangle.

So the rule is $\frac{n^2 - n}{2}$

Mathematics within the Whole Primary Curriculum

While there is much in mathematics that is intrinsically important and interesting in itself e.g. number patterns and sequences, it is strengthened by being seen within the wider context of the whole primary curriculum.

The so-called 'maths processes', including the strategies for problem-solving and investigations, are common to other areas of the curriculum. Children are involved in observing, experimenting, formulating, and testing theories in science; in collecting, classifying, and interrogating data in environmental studies; and in visualising, making, and modifying in craft and design. Children adopt an investigational approach to find out what happens when various objects are placed in a bucket of water, when paint of various colours is mixed, which media are most appropriate for making models for various purposes, or when helping to plan a school outing.

It would, therefore, seem proper to see mathematics as an integrated part of the primary curriculum, being used as a tool within other curricular areas. Such an approach would serve to strengthen mathematics, increasing understanding of the subject as a real and powerful tool which can be used in a wide variety of situations, as well as adding to the range, content, and understanding of what is already being done within those other subject areas:

> Measurement and symmetry arise frequently in art and craft; many patterns have a geometrical basis and designs may need enlarging or reducing. Environmental education makes use of measurement of many kinds and the study of maps introduces ideas of direction, scale and ratio. The patterns of the days of the week, of the calendar and of the recurring annual festivals all have a mathematical basis; for older children historical ideas require understanding of the passage of time, which can be illustrated on a 'time-line' which is analogous to the 'number - line' with which they will already be familiar. A great deal of measurement can arise in the course of simple cookery, including the calculation of cost; this may not always be straightforward if only part of a packet of ingredients has been used. Many athletic activities require measurement of distance and time. At the infant stage many stories and rhymes rely for their appeal on the pleasure of counting.

> W. Cockcroft, *Mathematics Counts* (para. 325)

It would be difficult to decide whether the following activity, described in *Towards a Problem-solving School* by Bob Smith, should be regarded as maths or science or craft and design.

> I think it will turn out a bit funny
> Why do you say that?
> Well average arms, average head and things.

Tom and his class of 10-year-olds had been set the problem of designing and making a 'machine' to measure parts of the body so that together they could produce a model of the average child. At the end of the early discussions on 'what to do' Tom had suddenly turned to me and offered this 'worry'. He seemed to have a vision of some alien being that would never be representative of the class. He wasn't the only person who was worried, but although the class was very hesitant about how they would tackle things, at least they could make a start on designing a machine.

First sketches and then mock-ups using cardboard were tried out in the classroom and then taken down to the workshop where the children were helped with choice of material and assembly techniques. Katie and Susan had designed a machine to measure 'all parts of the body'. The actual machine proved to be based on a 2-metre stick with sliding markers and was eventually used only for height. Nicola and Kath, on the other hand, had concentrated purely on a machine 'to measure round the head'.

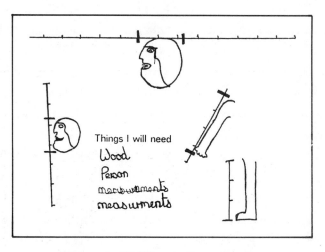

Figure 1: Children's first sketches

23 October: Class 1H

Three half days of the constructional work are over. This was to be evaluation/discussion. Katie and Susan began by demonstrating their machine and John and I then asked the class to comment. In particular we asked: what do you like about it? what don't you like about it? have you any suggestions for making it better? are there any faults?

The group liked the machine - in particular they thought it would be excellent to measure height. Tom didn't agree: he thought there was something wrong. 'It won't give the right height.'
'Why not?' demanded Susan.
'It starts at 5.'
'So. . .'
'So it'll be 5 out!'

Tom showed us where the stick fitted into the hole. Yes it did start at 5! The rest of the class murmured agreement. The makers were furious. Katie grabbed the stick away. 'Of course it will be right' she said. 'Look I'll take it out and measure you without the base - it'll be the same!' She did just that and the group could see the bottom of the stick was a zero. 'Yes but when the stick is in here. . .' and Tom grasped it back and put it in the hole . . . 'look it's at 5'.

'Yes but it's the same stick in or out!'

Tom was worried enough to sit down and the designers' reputations were intact!

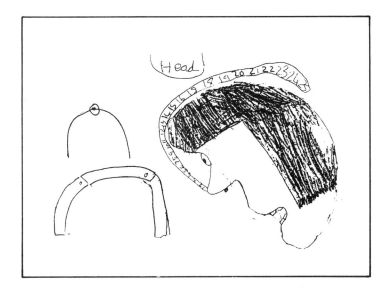

Figure 2: Machine 'to measure round the head'

The Isolation of Mathematics within the Primary Curriculum

A Separate Subject

Despite all this, mathematics tends to be taught as a separate subject and the cross-curricular links with respect to content and process are largely ignored.

Because children do not compartmentalise we have already moved away from teaching in isolation within subject boundaries such as history or geography. Rather we extract the essence of these curriculum areas from a theme. This approach can be very successful in motivating children and they become very involved in the learning; consequently, it is important to them. There is enormous scope for the English curriculum: children can report on visits, use study skills to research the chosen topic, write poems, stories, and plays. Similarly, science, history and geography, art and drama are usually drawn out of the overall theme or topic.

While it is common to find thematic work involving language, environmental studies, art and craft, the inclusion of maths is frequently of a minimal nature, often restricted to graphs and plans. Yet there is tremendous potential for meaningful learning to take place when mathematics is drawn out from a thematic structure. Involving children in situations where there is a real need for mathematics answers such questions as 'why are we doing this?' and 'what use is mathematics?'

A Different Teaching Style

Mathematics is not simply isolated by regarding it as a 'separate subject' but also in the way it is presented to children. In language, children are encouraged to develop their own ideas and express themselves in their own way. Similarly in environmental studies, children have scope to research their particular interests, to choose which avenues to follow and decide on the most appropriate way of relating their findings to others. It is much more unusual to find this approach in mathematics. Here, even teachers who are happy to work in a more child-centred manner in other curricular areas, tend to adopt a much more formal teacher-centred model ...a model in which the teacher has decided on a particular body of knowledge which must be delivered to all children in a particular way, taking little account of any method which the children may have developed for themselves. Yet children are very resourceful in developing methods which work for them.

As part of the PrIME Project, nearly 800 six and seven year olds started to work on the Calculator Aware Number Curriculum (CAN) in September 1986. In the report published at the end of the first year, *One Year of CAN - Reflections on a year's work*, there is a fascinating account of the variety of methods adopted by a class of six and seven year olds when asked to work out 28 + 29 in their heads and then tell how they had done it. The methods used included the following:

| 1 and 2 | Two children counted in ones, in different ways, using fingers |

3	30 + 30 = 60	30 - 29 = 1	30 - 28 = 2	1 + 2 = 3	60 - 3 = 57
4	8 + 9 = 17	20 + 20 = 40	40 + 17 = 57		
5	4 x 10 = 40	40 + 9 = 49	49 + 1 = 50	50 + 7 = 57	
6	25 + 25 = 50	4 + 3 = 7	50 + 7 = 57		
7	20 + 20 = 40	40 + 10 = 50	8 - 1 = 7	50 + 7 = 57	
8	20 + 20 = 40	9 + 8 = 17	17 = 10 + 7	40 + 10 = 50	50 + 7 = 57
9	20 + 20 = 40	9 + 8 = 17	17 is nearly 20	40 + 20 = 60	60 - 3 = 57
10	5 x 5 = 25	5 x 5 = 25	25 + 25 = 50	4 + 3 = 7	50 + 7 = 57
11	3 x 20 = 60	60 - 3 = 57			
12	29 + 10 = 39	39 + 10 = 49	49 + 8 = 57		

While clearly the teacher must make a decision about the curriculum content and has an obligation to all the children to help them towards an understanding of the important issues, the teacher must also be flexible and provide a variety of teaching/learning situations. A balance is needed between activities which are child-centred and those which are teacher-centred, between those which are child-initiated and those which are teacher-initiated, between collaborative work and individual work, between investigations and practice, between short-term and long-term activities, and between discussion, practical work and recording. By providing such a mixed diet, there is greater likelihood of all the children experiencing some success and the resulting confidence encouraging them in other areas.

Despite all the recommendations that mathematics teaching should provide a wide range of activities, the balance is still heavily in favour of exposition by the teacher, and the practice and consolidation of routines and skills. Problem-solving and investigational work are ignored or regarded as a fringe activity in very many classrooms.

Encouraging Problem-solving and Investigations in Mathematics

There are a variety of reasons why some teachers do not involve their children in problem-solving or investigational work. It may be that they:

- don't know where to start
- are worried about classroom organisation
- are unsure of how to develop this kind of work
- are anxious about record keeping
- are unsure of how to assess and evaluate this kind of work

Getting Started

Some investigations are very open-ended, others more closed. It may be best to start with a closed investigation and probably one initiated by the teacher rather than the children (see *New Technology in Primary Mathematics: INSET Resources*). For example:

1 Can you make all the numbers from 1 to 20 on your calculator using only the following keys

and using each key only once in each calculation?

2 You have red, blue and yellow pens. How many different striped flags can you make?

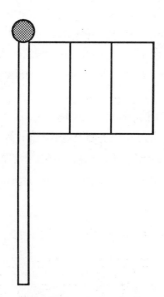

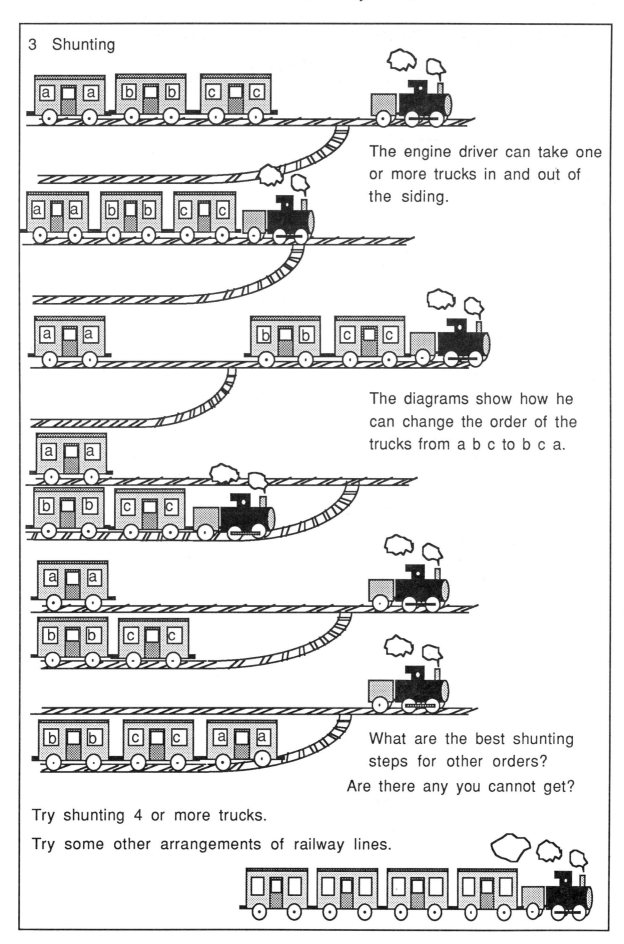

3 Shunting

The engine driver can take one or more trucks in and out of the siding.

The diagrams show how he can change the order of the trucks from a b c to b c a.

What are the best shunting steps for other orders?

Are there any you cannot get?

Try shunting 4 or more trucks.

Try some other arrangements of railway lines.

Classroom Organisation

If we want children to work independently, the classroom must be organised to facilitate this and the following issues need to be addressed:

- does the arrangement of the furniture lend itself to group work?
- is basic equipment on hand at all times?
- are the children trained to return equipment when they have finished with it?
- what size group are you going to work with - the whole class - one group - several groups - pairs - individuals?
- how is the group composition going to be decided - ability? friendship?
- do the children know what is expected of them?
- is time spent developing the children's self-discipline and self-assessment?
- do the children discuss with each other?
- do the children listen to each other?
- . . . .

Janette Warden's article in *Developing Mathematical Thinking*, entitled 'Making space for doing and talking with groups in the primary classroom' gives some useful ideas for organising the classroom to enable children to work in this way.

Developing Investigational Work

There are several stages to look out for when carrying out investigational work:

1 Outlining the task and determining the ground rules.
   In the example of the flags:
- need all 3 colours be used in each flag?
- can 2 strips of the same colour be next to each other?

2 Getting to grips with the task
- are the children tackling the task in a haphazard manner?
- are they adopting a logical approach?
- if it is the former, how are you going to develop the latter?

3 Recording
- are the children going to develop their own way of recording?
- are they going to be provided with ideas for recording?
- will it be a balance of these two?
- is a written record appropriate? if so, need it be words? would pictures or diagrams be more appropriate?
- would art, music, PE/movement or drama provide an alternative way of recording?

4   Coming up with a theory
- can the children explain what has happened?
- is there a pattern?
- how can the theory be tested? - did it work? - if not, why not? - will it always work?

5   Developing the investigation further
- what could be changed?

6   Coming to a conclusion
- what have the children found out?
- are there other ways of arriving at this conclusion?
- what next?

Record Keeping

It can be helpful to keep a record sheet for the investigations undertaken with such headings as:

- brief description of the investigation
- resources used
- teacher-initiated or child-initiated?
- grouping of children
- general strategies used by children
- concepts, skills and facts involved
- recording technique used
- unexpected developments
- surprises
- difficulties

If an individual child or group of children has produced a written record, a copy of this can be made and then annotated identifying the mathematical knowledge, skills and strategies being employed and where teacher input is needed to ensure further progression.

Evaluating the work

Evaluating the work is imperative and keeping records similar to those described above helps focus attention on:

- what you are doing
- why you are doing it
- how you are going about it
- what the mathematics is like
- where the children started from
- where they are now
- what next?

Behind the activity of investigations is the belief that an investigational approach will become part of a child's thinking, helping them to enjoy mathematics and learn more effectively. Wendy Garrard's report *I Don't Know, Let's Find Out* (Suffolk County Council) is full of useful ideas and thoughts about mathematical investigations in primary schools.

Developing Content through Problem-solving and Investigation

In language teaching in primary schools, children generally learn the tools of written language in context through creative writing or recording information. Similarly, the tools of mathematics - its facts, skills and concepts - can be developed through use in problem-solving and investigation. In the following activity, 'Playing PASSOLA', children adopt an investigative approach while developing a greater understanding of mathematical content.

Every child can succeed

Playing PASSOLA
by
Janet Hager

As headteacher of a very small primary school in Suffolk, I was aware of the need for my children to be involved with larger groups of children in other schools. It was in one such school visit that the children were introduced to the game of PASSOLA. This was the starting point for a series of mathematical investigations when we returned to our school.

Initially, the game involved a group of six children standing around in a ring with one of them holding a football. Then they played PASSOLA. The idea was that they passed the ball amongst themselves according to varying rules. In step 1 of six person PASSOLA, they passed the ball to the next person on their left so the path of the ball was something like this:

Start

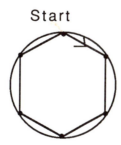

In step 2, they passed the ball to the next but one person on their left:

Start

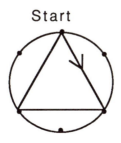

Then followed steps 3, 4, and 5:

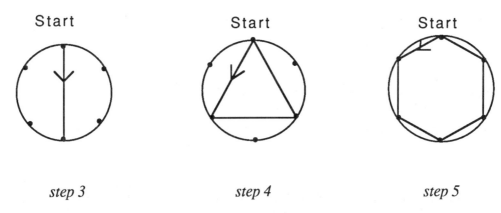

| *step 3* | *step 4* | *step 5* |

Moving on to seven-person PASSOLA, following the same sequences, more and varied shapes and patterns occur. For instance, step 3 of seven-person PASSOLA gives:

After this questions about *n* person PASSOLA, step *m* can be posed, such as: (a) predict patterns and shapes made; (b) work out which people will or will not receive the ball, and after how many passes; (c) state the relationship between *n* and *m* which determines whether or not all the people receive the ball.

At this stage I began to wonder how I could use and adapt the idea of PASSOLA in school so that all of the children, regardless of age or ability, could manage to succeed at some aspect of it.

I started with the idea of the throwing of a ball, giving the children plenty of opportunity to practise the skills involved. As all of us concerned with children know, there is always a minority who find even the most basic task difficult, and we were no exception! On many occasions the ball failed to reach its destination, bouncing and splashing in puddles in the playground. This, incidentally, led to unforeseen opportunities for investigations into environmental studies and science! Eventually we all agreed that if we sat down and rolled the ball to each other we would be more likely to achieve the required results.

Following on from ball throwing we went back into the classroom to commit to paper the shapes we had just made. All of the children were involved in drawing the patterns as accurately as possible, using rulers and sharp pencils (no rubbers!).

To make things easier each child was given printed sheets with dots representing the people. Then followed a number of discussions about these drawings for example:

What is the relationship between the number of lines and crossovers?
What is the relationship between the number of lines and number of angles?
Why were some patterns repeated? (The discussion is only limited by the imagination of the teacher.)

Each child, using a compass, was asked to draw several circles. Unfortunately, even after prolonged practice, there were still one or two who could manage no more than a rather uneven spiral, so plastic circles were brought into use. After all the children had drawn a circle of a given diameter on cardboard of varying thickness, they then proceeded to divide it into as many segments as people playing a game of PASSOLA.

All the children were given the opportunity to use protractors, calculators, Unifix bricks, beads, shells and even Smarties to make their calculations. (Beware of using Smarties except for the very strong willed - the results tended to be more inaccurate as temptation grew!)

This circle was then cut out (almost perfectly) and placed on another sheet of cardboard. Pencil marks were made wherever a radius reached the circumference (and those words were used when speaking to the children). After removing the circle, a needle was then pressed through the marks, leaving a number of holes. The children having a free choice of thread and needle size then transferred their drawn patterns in thread on to card. None of the children was given any help at this stage, apart from threading needles and tying knots. They all managed, regardless of age or ability, to reproduce their patterns perfectly.

Several of the older children then wanted to use some other medium to achieve a similar result, so art straws were introduced. But this posed another problem. If all of the straws used were the same length the finished shapes would vary enormously in size, so yet more calculations were needed to ensure a uniformity that the children themselves requested.

While this was going on, a discussion was developing amongst the younger children.

> It was good when I threw the ball and you dropped it.
> It made a big splash in that puddle.
> My mum will be mad when she sees my socks - they're new.
> Didn't the ball roll a long way? It made those wet lines go all over the place.
> They didn't make any shapes then! We should have kept on dropping it, so we didn't have to come in and do those drawings.

Then, after a pause.

> They must have made *some* shapes.
> Yes, some shapes, but not ones we can draw.
> We could if we saw where it went.
> Not if the water dried up we couldn't.

And so on.

We tried it again in the classroom. I suggested that the children threw the ball to each other and when it was dropped (or missed completely) we would watch to see where it went. After 10 minutes of frenetic activity and the most appalling throwing and catching ever seen in school, we decided to limit the space used to half of the classroom, and, to add interest, we soaked the ball in water before throwing it.

The next quarter of an hour needs no description! More rules were introduced. What would happen if the ball, which as every five-year-old knows is 'round', was confined within a circle? What shapes would we see? Trays and hoops were then brought into the activity.

Sheets of plain paper were placed under hoops and in trays and the balls rolled around at will, now soaked in paint. Perhaps the most startling of all the comments made by the children was by one of the youngest, who has specific learning difficulties:

> Look, look it's like magic. (Magic?)
> Look, this ball's round and the hoop's round, but look, look what's happened.
> I've got straight lines and corners all over the paper.

This alone leads to enough valuable language development to make the topic worthwhile.

While our attention was being given to this exciting discovery, another child found that if a tray is turned over so that there is no restraining edge, it is more difficult to control the path of the ball and it frequently falls off!

What emerges is a series of 'splots' in various colours across the classroom floor. The children, not quite believing their luck that their teacher not only was not reprimanding them but actually encouraging them in their task, set to work with a will. (Obviously this would need to be a playground activity in schools without washable floors.)

Paint-loaded tennis balls were dropped from knee level, waist level, shoulder level, head level and standing on tip-toe on a table level and, although the sizes and the number of splots varied, they all had certain characteristics in common. The first splot was large, the second was smaller, the third was smaller still. The third was closer to the second than the second was to the first, and so on along the path of the ball until there were continuous lines of paint (usually appearing under the piano) where the ball stopped bouncing.

What opportunities there were then for innumerable measuring activities using such diverse materials as measures, rulers, Cuisenaire rods, shoes, handspans, etc. And what problems there were when deciding where the actual measurement should start and finish. Should we begin at the centre of the splot or from the edge? Where did the edge begin? Where did it end? The amount of mathematical, scientific, and creative investigation which came from an apparently simple activity was endless, limited only by the amount of time available.

Our investigations took place over a period of several weeks, providing a source for much exciting work, and even then we had by no means exhausted all the possibilites.

PASSOLA - Getting Started

We need 7 people standing in a circle

- evenly spaced

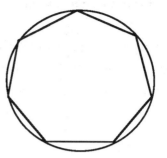

Is it a circle?

How do we get it to be equally spaced?

We're going to play PASSOLA. This is 7-person PASSOLA.

Pass the ball to the next person. This is PASSOLA 7 1 - 7 people step 1

Stop when you want to.

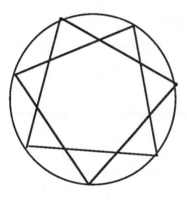

Try   PASSOLA 7 2

            PASSOLA 7 3

            PASSOLA 7 4

            PASSOLA 7 5

            PASSOLA 7 6

            PASSOLA 7 8

Do we need any other rules?

How do we decide when to stop?

Can you 'image' the patterns?

Use wool to trace out the patterns

Figure 1: Starting with PASSOLA

This is class SJ
playing passola 7 step 1

Passola

This morning we played Passola in the hall. First we did 7 step 1. We just threw the ball to each other around a circle of 7 people. Then we did 7 step 2. With this one we threw the ball to every other person. This time the ball went round the circle twice. Then we did 7 step 3. With this one we missed two people out and we went round three times. The people in my group then did 7 step 4. It was the same as 7 step 3 except we threw the ball the other way. Next we did 7 step 5. That was the same as 7 step 2 but we threw the ball in the opposite direction as well. Then we did 7 step 6 that also was the same as 7 step 1 but in the other direction. We didn't do 7 step 7 because the ball wouldn't make any pattern. We made shapes. The shapes were nonagons, triangles Heptagons and quadrilaterals How we knew where to stop was when the ball got to the person who started with it. Every time no matter which step we did it always would draw 7 points on the circle. Here is a diagram

7 Step 2 ⬡ start

Triangles ✓   Passola 7-3
Quadrilaterals .
Heptagon ✱

Figure 2: Children's recording of PASSOLA

39

PASSOLA - Moving On

Try PASSOLA with different numbers of people

What's the same?

What's different?

Can you predict?

What shapes can you make?

Try PASSOLA 8 2

What shape is created?

Sit down if you're not involved

What will:

    PASSOLA 100 99

    PASSOLA 100 1

    PASSOLA 100 50 be?

Can you record the patterns?

How do you draw 6 points
around a circle?

    What strategies do you use?

      What order?

  Opposites?   Symmetry?

How does this differ for 7 points?

Did you make use of:
    a protractor

      360 degrees in a circle
      6 points so every 60 degrees
      5 points so every . . .

    the constant button on a calculator
      6 points . . . 60, 120, 180, 240
      5 points . . .

LOGO

```
TO PASSOLA :PEOPLE :STEP
REPEAT :PEOPLE [FD 200  RT 360 * :STEP / :PEOPLE]
END
```

Figure 3: Developing PASSOLA

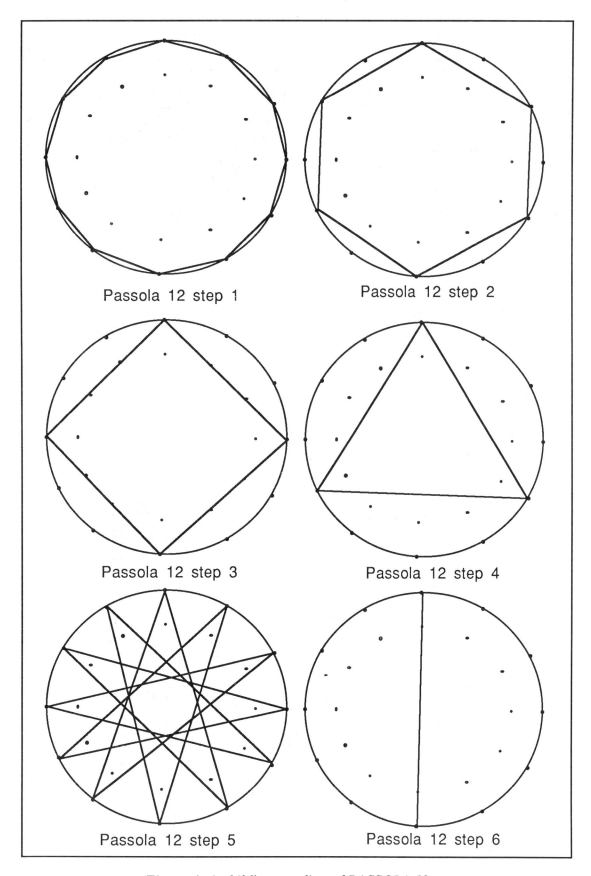

Passola 12 step 1

Passola 12 step 2

Passola 12 step 3

Passola 12 step 4

Passola 12 step 5

Passola 12 step 6

Figure 4: A child's recording of PASSOLA 12

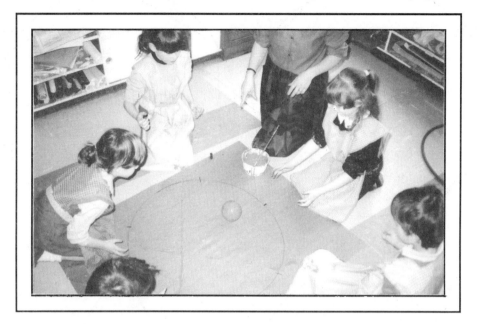

The children passed a ball covered in paint to each other.

Paint was used to make a more permanent record of the path taken by the ball.

PASSOLA - Resources

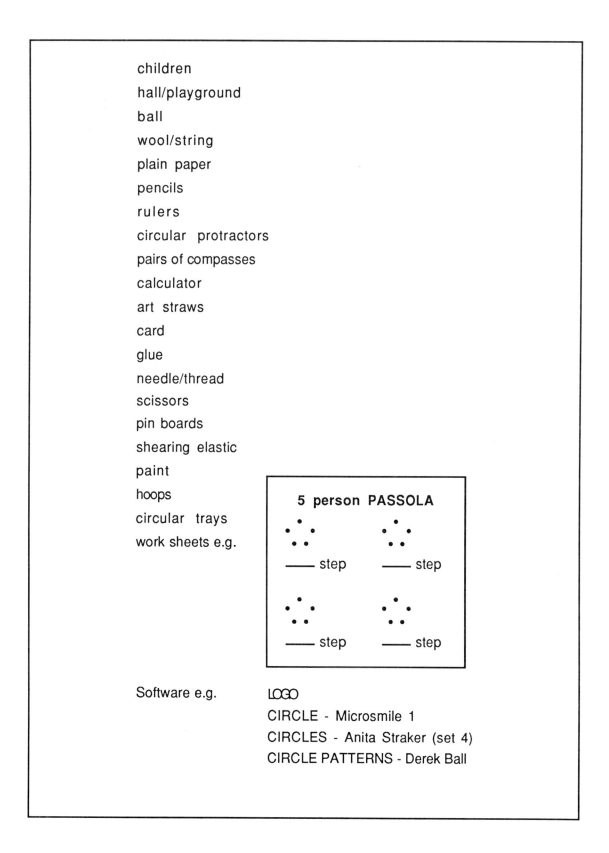

children
hall/playground
ball
wool/string
plain paper
pencils
rulers
circular protractors
pairs of compasses
calculator
art straws
card
glue
needle/thread
scissors
pin boards
shearing elastic
paint
hoops
circular trays
work sheets e.g.

5 person PASSOLA

—— step   —— step

—— step   —— step

Software e.g.

LOGO
CIRCLE - Microsmile 1
CIRCLES - Anita Straker (set 4)
CIRCLE PATTERNS - Derek Ball

Figure 5: 'Shopping list' for PASSOLA

String and polystyrene tiles helped these children to recreate their pattern

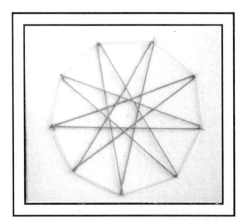

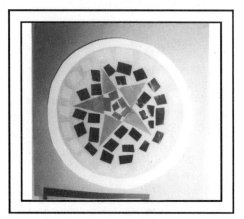

PASSOLA 9 1 and 9 4   *A sticky paper PASSOLA mosaic*

A display of PASSOLA work from one class

PASSOLA - Identifying the Mathematics Content and Processes

A teacher, reflecting on the work which her class of second and third year juniors had done with PASSOLA and trying to identify the mathematics content and processes that had taken place, wrote:

> In the initial stages the children were estimating as they set up the circles, predicting what patterns would merge and then testing as they worked out who to throw the ball to. In the classroom they then needed to measure length, use pairs of compasses to draw circles and develop a strategy for spacing dots around the circumference which gave me an opportunity to show the children how to use a protractor. They then had to decide how many units were needed to make a complete turn. The children all knew 'right ninety' from their use of Logo and soon worked out that four right angles were needed and it did not take long for one child to decide she must divide the four right angles by the number of dots needed. They had been rounding up to the nearest penny in a recent session and so the children were quite happy to accept 360 divided by 7 was about 52. After the PASSOLA drawings were made, shapes inside the drawings were classified and listed. The children then wanted to know what the shape with a curved edge was and fractions of a circle were discussed. One child did PASSOLA nine step four and was delighted to find a nonagon at the centre.

Content	**Processes**
Measurement	Describing
Symmetry	Defining
Angle	Classifying (2D shapes)
Properties of a circle	Approximating
Protractor/compass work	Looking for pattern
2D shapes	Predicting
Modular arithmetic	Testing
Notation	Generalising
Number patterns	:
Fractions	:
Multiples and factors	:
Points/lines/position	:
Calculator work	:
Algorithms . . . programming	:
:	:
:	:
:	:
:	:

Developing Mathematics within Cross-Curricular Themes

> When the use of class teachers is the norm, as in primary schools, it is the responsibility of each individual teacher to ensure that mathematics is used where appropriate opportunities occur. At all times there should be a positive approach to the wide use of mathematics through the curriculum. If mathematics is not seen to be needed or used explicitly in project work and in other subjects within the curriculum then the claim that mathematics is a useful subject must sound rather hollow to the pupils.
>
> DES, *Mathematics from 5 - 16*

The opportunities for developing mathematics from an integrated theme can be very exciting for both teacher and child. Most schools, however, choose to use one of the published mathematics schemes. While these provide structure, continuity, and balance they tend to treat mathematics as a separate entity. Working through a scheme can become an inhibitor of quality mathematics teaching and undermine a teacher's professional judgment.\Teachers who lack confidence in mathematics tend to think that 'the scheme knows best' and they can let it take over the responsibility of their children's mathematical development.⁄Drawing mathematics from a theme can add breadth and depth to the curriculum based on a published scheme.

Difficulties of Working Thematically

There are many teachers who, although they would like to include mathematics in their project or topic work, do not find it easy to identify the mathematics in other areas of the curriculum. Pressure of work in the classroom makes it particularly difficult to ensure that advantage is taken of mathematical opportunities when they arise in other curriculum areas. When planning activities, especially any topic or thematic work, it is therefore necessary for the teacher to try to identify at the outset the mathematical possibilities which exist within planned work. While not all of these will necessarily be realised, planning in this way makes it easier for the teacher to take advantage of the opportunities when they arise in a busy classroom.

Other difficulties lie in ensuring that the mathematics, once identified, is at an appropriate level for the children's intellectual abilities, that it is fully developed and that there is no more than an appropriate amount of repetition. An integral part of this work will be a record of the processes a child has experienced, an assessment of the concepts, facts and skills acquired together with a pointer to future developments. Such a record is very important. Not only does it help teachers to evaluate the work but also to justify the work to parents and colleagues and relate it to the mathematics scheme when necessary.

Advantages of Working Thematically

The benefits of working thematically outweigh difficulties as teachers have recognised in their work in other specialist areas such as language and environmental studies. A thematic approach:

- enables mathematics to be seen in a broader context

- develops links between mathematics and other curriculum areas

- provides a reason for developing particular aspects of mathematics

- involves staff with a variety of areas of expertise when adopted throughout a school

- gives an opportunity for an extended piece of work

- provides a focus to which children can bring their own experiences

- acts as a stimulus for children to ask their own questions

- encourages independent learning

- alters children's perceptions of mathematics . . . they see that mathematics has applications in the real world

- provides a vehicle for the development of mathematical processes

- makes better use of resources

- gives scope for a variety of learning/teaching situations . . . individual, group, and class work . . . child initiated and/or teacher initiated stimulus and exploration

- gives teachers a chance to respond to individual children's needs, levels of understanding and range of abilities.

Getting Started with a Thematic Approach

The relationship between themes and the mathematics curriculum can be illustrated by the following diagram:

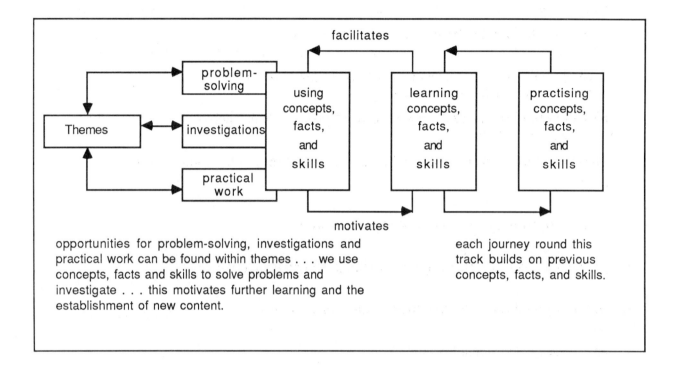

Figure 1: The relationship between themes and the mathematical curriculum

The approach to teaching mathematics via themes could well be a new and daunting challenge to many teachers. But there is no need to take everything on board at once. We can start anywhere and proceed at a pace with which we feel comfortable.

Teachers sold on teaching and practising skills will begin on the right-hand side of the diagram. For these teachers a small excursion into problem-solving, investigative, or practical work, which need not initially be related to a theme, may be sufficient. The resulting enjoyment and success should encourage them to spend more time in this area . . . perhaps linking an investigation to an overall theme . . . perhaps developing a specific mathematical concept or skill within a theme. Since mathematical processes are developed by applying mathematical concepts, facts, and skills in problem-solving and investigation, a shift towards the left-hand side of the diagram will involve the teachers in process as well as content, resulting in a growing awareness of a balanced mathematics diet.

When identifying the mathematics within a theme or topic, there are several questions which teachers need to ask themselves. They include:

- is the mathematics within a theme suitable for the children's present levels of understanding, skills and experience?
- do I really know the children's levels in these areas?
- is the theme going to give the children an opportunity to encounter a new skill when there is a real need to use it?
- are the children going to come to understanding a new concept by meeting it in a relevant context?
- is there opportunity for teaching concepts and skills?
- am I in danger of stopping the flow of or interest in the theme by including too many 'teaching interludes'?

Cross-curricular Themes with Varying Mathematical Content

A flexible approach to teaching mathematics should include some work developed from themes. Ideally these themes should give opportunities to apply concepts, facts and skills and to develop processes. Some cross-curricular themes have greater mathematical potential than others.

There are themes with a high mathematical content which are chosen primarily to develop particular mathematical ideas. Number squares or Spirals would be examples of such themes.

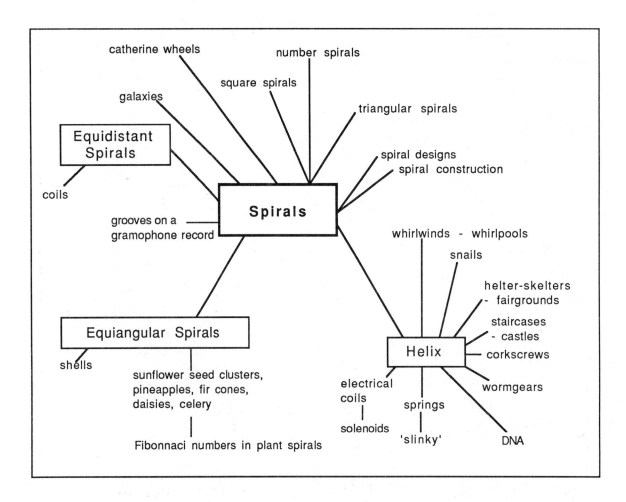

Figure 1: Topic web for 'Spirals'

Other themes have substantial mathematical content and also give scope for much work in other areas of the curriculum. Themes such as Enclosing, Balance, or Pathways would fit into this group.

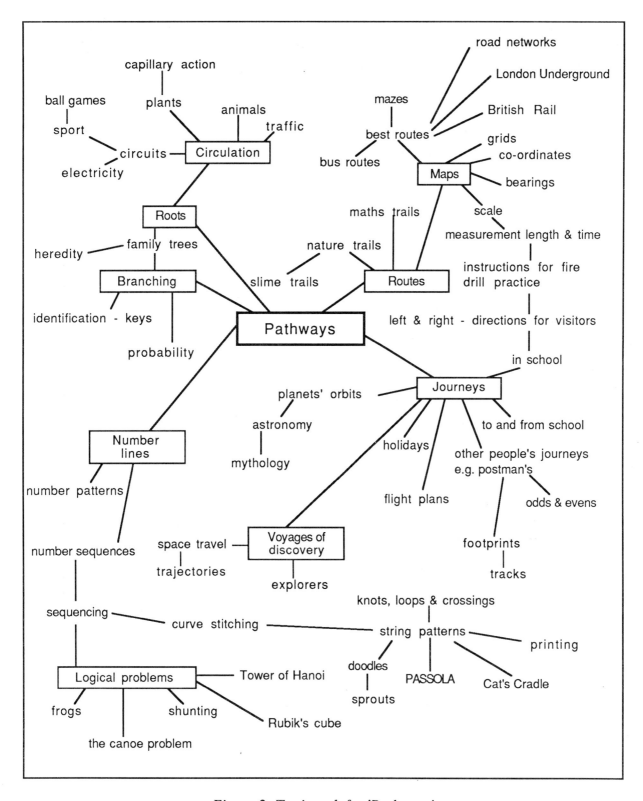

Figure 2: Topic web for 'Pathways'

There are themes with a relatively small mathematical content which are chosen because of the opportunities to develop ideas in other curriculum areas. Owls or My Midnight World would fit into this category.

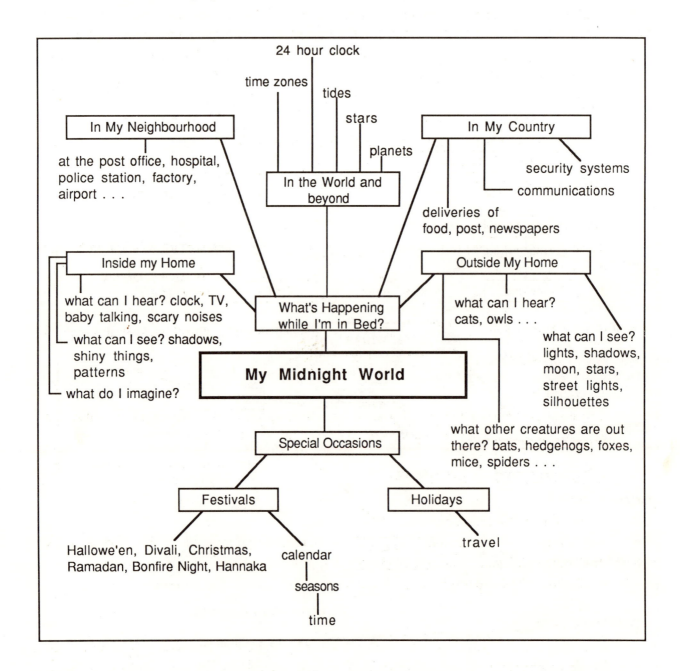

Figure 3: Topic web for 'My Midnight World'

The Contribution of New Technology

Calculators and computers are powerful tools in a thematic approach. Not only can they be used to develop problem-solving and investigations, but they can also be extremely useful in linking mathematics across the primary curriculum. Calculators can be used to widen the range of number investigations. They also enable children to manipulate very large numbers and decimal numbers allowing them to use their mathematics in 'real life' situations. Categories of software are discussed fully in *The Impact of New Technology on the Primary Mathematics Curriculum* booklet. Briefly, there are open-ended software tools and software which contains an embedded problem.

Software containing embedded problems includes:

Specific investigations
These are smaller programs which pose a specific problem and require children to collect data for analysis and generalisation.

Adventures
Good adventure games involve children in decision making and problem-solving along a path to an end goal.

Simulations
These are programs which enable children to model a 'real' situation which for a variety of reasons is inaccessible to them in their daily lives.

Open ended software tools include:

Databases and spreadsheets
These are used to store, retrieve, sort, and search through large quantities of data. They involve the children in collecting, classifying, and interrogating data. Most packages have the facility to display results in graphical form.

Logo
This is a creative and flexible tool for developing children's mathematical thinking. In 'control technology', Logo is widely used to control models which children have designed and built themselves.

Graphics packages
Some graphics packages allow patterns to be created by designing and tessellating tiles, while others provide the facility to draw and paint freely on the screen.

The following chart indicates possible ways in which the computer could be used to develop the themes already described.

		SPIRALS	PATHWAYS	MY MIDNIGHT WORLD
S O F T W A R E C O N T A I N I N G E M B E D D E D P R O B L E M S	**Specific Investigations**	Spirals DOGS (Teaching with a Micro 3) SPLOT (Teaching with a Micro 3) SPIRALS (First 30 SMILE) Number Patters with Spirals ENGRAM (Teaching with a Micro 3) Curves of Pursuit PURSUIT (Maths with a Micro 2)	Co-ordinates ELEPHANT (first 30 SMILE) RHINO (First 30 SMILE) ISLAND YACHT RACE (The Sea - Fernleaf) Grids ROUTES (Maths 9-13 MEP) PLOD (Teaching with a Micro 1) Compass Points PILOT (First 30 SMILE) Mazes MAZE (First 30 SMILE) 3D MAZE (Next 17 SMILE) Chord Patterns CIRCLES (Maths 9-13 MEP) CIRCLE (First 30 SMILE) Number Patterns MONTY (SLIMWAM 2) COUNTER (SLIMWAM 2) Logic Puzzles -movement BOAT (First 30 SMILE) TADPOLES (Next 17 SMILE) JUMBO (Infant Pack MEP)	
	Adventures (with a mathematical flavour)		PUFF (A. Straker) LITTLE RED RIDING HOOD (Selective Software) KINGDOM OF HELIOR (Longman) MARTELLO TOWER (A. Straker) 'L' - A MATHEMATICAL ADVENTURE (ATM)	LOST OWLS (MAPE Owl Pack)
	Simulations		CARS - MATHS IN MOTION (CSH) FLIGHT PATH (Storm Ed.) ROADS (Fernleaf) CANAL BUILDER (AUP) QUICK CARTAGE CO. (Wiley)	SUBURBAN FOX (Ginn) PIPISTRELLE (MESU)

Figure 1: Software containing embedded problems

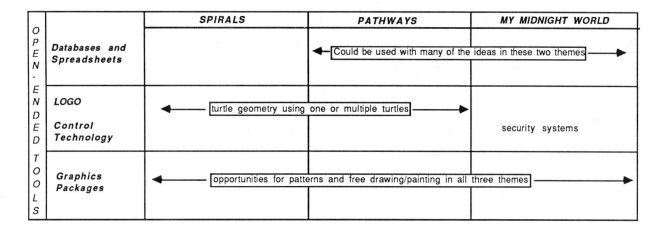

		SPIRALS	PATHWAYS	MY MIDNIGHT WORLD
O P E N - E N D E D T O O L S	Databases and Spreadsheets		← Could be used with many of the ideas in these two themes →	
	LOGO Control Technology	← turtle geometry using one or multiple turtles →		security systems
	Graphics Packages	← opportunities for patterns and free drawing/painting in all three themes →		

Figure 2: Open-ended software tools

It could be argued that adopting a thematic approach to mathematics is challenging enough without bring new technology into it. Certainly it would not be possible to take everything on board at once. Some teachers have started by using a few smaller investigative programs or by working with an adventure. Others have started by familiarising themselves with one open-ended application, e.g. a database, and using it extensively in a variety of contexts.

For many teachers the micro has been the tool which has instigated and facilitated group work and has helped them make a start towards developing an investigative approach to mathematics. The use of adventures, simulations, graphics packages and databases provides avenues to link and develop mathematics in other curriculum areas. Generally speaking, children are highly motivated by new technology and respond well to the opportunities it offers to become independent learners. For all these reasons, new technology can be said to have made us reassess our role as teachers and our perceptions of mathematics and its place in the primary curriculum.

Bibliography

APU	*Mathematical Performance Primary Survey Reports 1 - 3*	HMSO, 1981, 1982, 1983
W. Cockcroft	*Mathematics Counts (Cockcroft Report)*	HMSO, 1981
Education and Science, Department of	*Mathematics From 5 to 16*	HMSO, 1985
R. Fisher (Ed.) (L. Burton)	*Problem-solving in Primary Schools*	Basil Blackwell, 1987
A. Floyd	*Developing Mathematical Thinking*	Addison Wesley 1981
W. Garrard	*I Don't Know, Let's Find Out*	Suffolk County Council, 1986
K. M. Hart	*Concepts in Secondary Mathematics & Science Project*	Murray, 1981
J. Holt	*How Children Learn*	Pelican, 1983
M.M. Lindquist. et al,	*The Third National Mathematics Assessment: results and implications for elementary and middle schools*	Arithmetic Teacher 31 (4), 1983
PrIME Project Team	*One Year of CAN*	PrIME, 1988
H. Shuard	*Primary Mathematics Today and Tomorrow*	Longmans (SCDC), 1986
R. Smith	*Towards a Problem-solving School*	Maths Teaching, 112, September 1985

Software Resources

SPIRALS, ELEPHANTS, RHINO, PILOT, MAZE, CIRCLE, BOAT	First 30 - SMILE Programs (ILEA)
3D MAZE, TADPOLES	Next 17 - SMILE Programs (ILEA)
PLOD	Teaching with a Micro 1 (Shell Centre)
DOGS, SPLOT, ENGRAM	Teaching with a Micro 3 (Shell Centre)
PURSUIT	Maths with a Micro (RDLU)
ROUTES, CIRCLES	Maths 9 - 13 (MEP)
MONTY, COUNTER	Slimwam 2 (ATM)
THE SEA, ROADS	Fernleaf
PUFF, MARTELLO TOWER	Anita Straker
LITTLE RED RIDING HOOD	Selective Software
KINGDOM OF HELIOR	Longman
'L' - A MATHEMATICAL ADVENTURE	ATM
CARS - MATHS IN MOTION	Cambridge Software House
JUMBO	Infant Pack (MEP)
SUBURBAN FOX	Ginn
LOST OWLS	MAPE Owl Pack
PIPISTRELLE, BRANCH	MESU
FLIGHT PATH	Storm Education
CANAL BUILDER	AVP
QUICK CARTAGE CO.	Wiley

Databases

OURFACTS	MESU
BRANCH	MESU
INFORM	Resource
GRASS	Newman College
QUEST	Advisory Unit

Spreadsheets

VIEWSHEET	Acornsoft
GRASSHOPPER	Newman College
MULTIPLAN	Research machines
PSS	Cambridge Software House
LOGISTIX	Grafox

Logo

Logotron Logo	
Archimedes Logo	Logotron
480Z LogoResearch Machines	
Nimbus Logo	Research Machines

Control Technology

Control Logo	Logotron
LEGO Control Logo	LEGO
Control Logo	Research Machines
CONTACT	MESU

Graphics Packages

TESSELLATIONS	Cambridge University Press
MOSAIC	Advisory Unit
PAINTSPA	SPA
IMAGE	Homerton College
TAKE HALF	First 30 SMILE Programs (ILEA)
NEWTILES	Next 17 SMILE Programs (ILEA)
TILEKIT	Slimwam 2 - ATM